EDWARD JAMES OLMOS

MEXICAN-AMERICAN ACTOR

ELIZABETH COONROD MARTINEZ

Hispanic Heritage
The Millbrook Press
Brookfield, Connecticut

Facing page: Edward James Olmos holds an Emmy Award for his role in the television series, Miami Vice.

Library of Congress Cataloging-in-Publication Data
Martinez, Elizabeth Coonrod, 1954–
Edward James Olmos : Mexican-American actor /
by Elizabeth Coonrod Martinez.
p. cm.—(Hispanic heritage)
Includes bibliographical references and index.
Summary: Tells the life story of Mexican-American actor
Edward James Olmos, emphasizing how he used his Chicano
background as a resource for his art and his commitment
to bringing integrity to portrayals of Latinos.
ISBN 1-56294-410-X (lib. bdg.)
1. Olmos, Edward James—Juvenile literature.   2. Actors—United
States—Biography—Juvenile literature.   3. Mexican Americans—
Biography.   [1. Olmos, Edward James.   2. Actors and actresses.
3. Mexican Americans—Biography.]   I. Title.   II. Series.
PN2287.O438M37   1994
792′.028′092—dc20   [B]   93-37659   CIP   AC

Cover photo courtesy © Frederic De La Fosse, Sygma

Photos courtesy of AP/Wide World Photos: pp. 3, 12, 14, 22, 26;
Gamma Liaison: pp. 4 (D. Burrows), 17 (Susan Greenwood), 18
(B. King), 21, 24 (D. Burrows), 25, 28 (A. Berliner); Schalkwiji/
Art Resource, New York: p. 7; UPI/Bettmann: pp. 9, 19.

Published by The Millbrook Press
2 Old New Milford Road
Brookfield, Connecticut 06804

EDWARD JAMES OLMOS

East Los Angeles, California, a mostly Mexican-American area, was Edward James Olmos's home. Life there taught him about acting. Here a colorful mural by young Mexican-Americans decorates an East L.A. building.

For *Edward James Olmos*, East Los Angeles, California, was like a theater. Many of the people who lived there seemed to be acting—especially the boys. A rule that nobody made but that a lot of boys obeyed said that if you were a *Chicano*—a male of Mexican background—you had to act tough. (*Chicano* is a shortened form of the Spanish word for Mexican, *Mexicano*.)

In the 1940s, around the time Eddie—as Olmos was known to his family and friends—was born, acting tough for Chicanos meant wearing a suit with a long coat that reached to the knees, a "zoot suit." Many years later, in the 1970s and 1980s, some Chicanos acted tough in a different way. They belonged to gangs and wore clothes that had special gang colors. Chicano gangs fought among themselves and with other gangs to see which ones were the toughest. Often members wound up in jail or dead.

Eddie had much in common with other Chicano boys of both generations. Like them, he was born in East Los Angeles (L.A.). And like them, he acted. But Eddie acted in movies, in plays, and on television. East L.A. was his first acting school. He took what he experienced living there and being a Chicano and turned it into art.

Through his work on-screen and off-screen, Edward James Olmos demonstrated that being a Chicano could mean being creative and strong. He showed that being a Chicano was more than simply acting tough—especially in ways that destroyed people. Edward James Olmos became a great actor and a great representative of Latino people. This is his story.

BASEBALL AND ROCK & ROLL · Eddie's father, Pedro Olmos, came from a family of thirteen in Mexico City. Pedro's father and uncle had fought in the Mexican Revolution, a war that overthrew the Mexican dictator Porfirio Díaz.

Eddie's mother, Eleanor Huizar Olmos, was born in Los Angeles, where her parents were also born. During World War II she went to visit her sister, who was studying in Mexico City. There she met Pedro, who was running a business that he had started when he was fourteen years old.

Pedro fell in love with Eleanor and followed her back to Los Angeles. He got a job and then convinced Eleanor to marry him. Eddie was their second child, born on February 24, 1947, in the Boyle Heights neighborhood of East Los Angeles.

*This mural by Mexican painter David Siqueiros shows
Mexicans going to war during the 1910 Mexican Revolution.
Edward James Olmos's grandfather and great uncle fought
in this war to end unfair government in Mexico.*

When Eddie Olmos was seven, he moved with his parents, older brother, and younger sister to another neighborhood in East L.A. There he discovered baseball. He began by watching and playing sockball—a game played with a tennis ball wrapped inside a sock. Later he got a real softball and played on teams. Eddie wasn't really talented, he later said. But he knew how to watch and learn, and he learned the game better than almost anyone else he played with. Eddie felt proud when his dad came to watch his games at Montebello ballpark. During the winters some members of the Los Angeles Dodgers would come to this park to work out. One day they even asked Eddie to be their catcher during a workout.

Eddie's parents divorced when he was eight. Sometimes when he felt sad he would force himself to play baseball, and then he felt better. This discipline became a habit that helped him when he began acting.

On the weekends, Eddie and his sister would visit their dad and listen to his favorite music on the radio. Among his dad's favorite dances were the jitterbug and the mambo. Eddie wanted to learn how to do them so he asked his dad if he would teach him and his sister. Pretty soon they were dancing the mambo and the jitterbug every weekend in his dad's kitchen. Eddie liked dancing so much that he decided he wanted to sing and dance when he grew up.

Eddie turned thirteen in 1960, when performers such as Little Richard and others were becoming famous for playing rock and roll. He started listening to music as much as he played baseball. He liked to imitate the singers he heard, using some of the dance steps he had learned from his dad. It was fun. And Eddie discovered that other kids liked to watch him.

By his senior year in high school, Eddie was singing in a rock and roll band that rehearsed in his friends' garages. The band played at parties, and by the time he graduated from Montebello High School in 1964, Eddie earned a living from music. "I wasn't a great singer," he admitted, "but I knew how to have *style*, how to show off your personality." Eddie would sing and dance, and the audience would cheer.

Edward James Olmos's father was not alone in his love of the jitterbug and the mambo. These dances were popular worldwide in the 1950s. Here dancers mambo at West Germany's International Jitterbug and Mambo Contest.

He formed a band called The Pacific Ocean with his friend Denny Dias, a guitar player. For four years the band played at a famous club called Gazzarri's, on the

Sunset Strip in Los Angeles. It performed all kinds of music—jazz, rhythm and blues, folk and country, and rock and roll.

In 1968, Eddie's group was hired as the regular band at a club in Los Angeles called The Factory, where movie stars were members. That summer the band also played free shows for Robert Kennedy's presidential campaign.

COLLEGE AND ACTING · Eddie was also going to college while he had his band. He attended East Los Angeles College from 1964 to 1966, and California State University, Los Angeles, from 1966 to 1968. At first he studied psychology, the science of how people think and act, and criminology, the science of crime. Later, he majored in dance and theater.

Eddie used to do his homework on his breaks between performances. People thought he was crazy to work so hard, but he knew he wanted to have a college education so that he could get ahead. He said, "I didn't know where I wanted to be, but I knew I would get there faster if I went to college."

One evening at The Factory, a young woman named Kaija was sitting in the audience. Eddie saw her and instantly fell in love. Her father was the famous actor Howard Keel, but Eddie didn't let that bother him. They dated, and were married a year later.

After he married Kaija, Eddie quit his band and started looking for acting jobs. He did a lot of small parts in plays and television shows, and he also made a movie in Spanish called *¡El Alambrista!* (Spanish for "tightrope artist"). The movie, about the difficult life of illegal immigrants, won the Golden Camera Prize at the International Cannes Film Festival in France in 1977.

The following year Eddie got a big break. He was chosen for the lead role in a play called *Zoot Suit.* It was written by another Latino from Los Angeles, Luis Valdez. Eddie played the part of El Pachuco, a Mexican American from East L.A.

To portray this character, Eddie drew on what the older generations of Chicano "actors" had done in the "theater" of his youth—the 1940s East L.A. streets. These Mexican Americans had dressed in zoot suits, just like Eddie's character in the play. The suits, also called "drape shapes" because of their bagginess, were more than just a fashion. They became symbols that meant many things to many people.

A series of clashes called the "Zoot Suit Wars" took place in 1943. In 1942, twenty-four Mexican-American "Zooters" were arrested for the murder of a young man. Although the Mexican Americans were cleared of those charges against them, some local residents and police officers believed they—and nearly all Zooters—were troublemakers. During the summer of 1943, L.A.

teenagers—joined by U.S. servicemen—fought with groups of Zooters. In one incident, several thousand servicemen and civilians entered Mexican-American neighborhoods and beat all the Zooters they could find. Reports suggested that some police officers, rather than breaking up the fighting, joined in.

Because of the Zoot Suit Wars, Zooters went down in L.A. history. Eddie researched every aspect of their behavior for his role in *Zoot Suit*.

The play was a success in Los Angeles. Eddie was nominated for a prestigious Tony Award, given for acting in the theater. And he also received the Los Angeles Drama Critics Circle Award for Best Actor in 1978.

In 1979 the play moved to New York City. Eddie arrived in New York and went straight to the Winter Garden Theater, where he would perform. Only the janitor was there, and the stage was dark. Eddie turned

A police officer poses a young Chicano Zooter arrested during the Zoot Suit Wars for a mug shot.

on the lights and walked up on the stage where stars had performed. He had dreamed that someday he would also be there. Suddenly he sank to his knees, overcome with emotion. He was in New York, and it was the happiest moment of his life.

His being in a play in New York City made many people in the television and movie business notice Eddie. After the play ended in New York, he went back to his home in Los Angeles. He had money, and he knew something about himself now. He didn't want to do just any kind of acting job. He wanted to play a part that would make people think or inspire them. But for the next few years, movie and television producers offered him leading parts in which he would have to play a Latino who was a criminal, drug addict, rapist, corrupt politician, or other bad guy. Eddie wouldn't do it. For a while, he turned down lots of money, because he refused to act the part of a bad person who didn't inspire anyone.

PORTRAYING MEXICAN EXPERIENCE · In 1982 the Public Broadcasting System (PBS) asked Olmos to star in a TV movie about a real event that happened in Texas in 1900. It was about a Mexican cowhand named Gregorio Cortez.

Olmos liked playing the role in this movie, *The Ballad of Gregorio Cortez*, more than any he had ever performed, because the character had integrity. He stood up for what he knew was right even when other people treated him unfairly.

Olmos worked hard on this movie. He researched, read, and studied about Gregorio Cortez. He also wrote all of the music for the movie, putting the information he had learned into the songs.

When the movie was finished and aired on PBS television, Olmos was proud because it was a very good movie. He also wanted more people to see it, so he spent the next two years traveling all around the country to help promote the movie in local theaters.

Edward James Olmos as Gregorio Cortez. "It was the biggest man-hunt . . . at the beginning of the twentieth century," said Olmos of the hunt for the Mexican ranch hand forced to be an outlaw.

GREGORIO CORTEZ

Gregorio Cortez and his brother Romaldo were Mexican-born ranch hands. In 1900 they moved to Karnes County, Texas, and started a farm. In June of that year, the county sheriff came to the farm. He was looking for horse thieves and thought Romaldo might be one of them.

The sheriff couldn't speak Spanish and brought a man who knew only a little of the language. When the sheriff questioned Romaldo, the interpreter couldn't understand the answers. The sheriff grew confused and suspicious. He decided to arrest Romaldo and pulled out his gun. When Romaldo, who was unarmed, tried to stop him, the sheriff fired—and killed Romaldo. Gregorio, who was present, took out his gun. The sheriff fired at Gregorio. He shot back and killed the sheriff.

The next day Gregorio fled the farm. He believed he was right to defend himself and his brother, but he knew Texans would not believe a Mexican was right. After a ten-day chase, Texas Rangers captured him. Gregorio stood trial for murder eleven times, being found innocent at one trial and guilty at the next. He was finally declared guilty—not of murdering the sheriff, but of murdering someone else when he was on the run. The governor of Texas pardoned him in 1913, and he was set free, after spending one third of his life in jail. He died three years later.

Mexicans on both sides of the border saw Gregorio Cortez as a man who fought for his rights. His story was passed from one generation to the next. Today it is a legend.

MIAMI VICE · Then something happened that would make Edward James Olmos famous all around the country. In 1984 the producer of a new television police show, *Miami Vice*, thought Olmos's personality was perfect for the part of a police lieutenant. Olmos agreed and moved to Miami, where the show was made. From then on Olmos's character, Lieutenant Martin Castillo, became an important part of the *Miami Vice* series. He was the serious, thoughtful boss of the police detectives Crockett (played by Don Johnson) and Tubbs (played by Philip Michael Thomas).

Olmos came on the series in its fifth week. The producer and Eddie worked together to decide what kind of person this police boss was going to be. On each show, viewers found out new things about the tough Lieutenant Castillo. He spoke eight languages, five of them Asian. He had Ninja training, which was what gave him self-confidence. And something tragic had happened in his past life. By the thirteenth show, people found out that Lieutenant Castillo had lost his family in a shoot-out between police and drug traffickers. The *Miami Vice* fans started feeling close to the man Eddie portrayed. He became an example of someone who had both pain and courage—a hero.

In the second year of *Miami Vice*, Olmos directed an episode titled "Bushido." Many people said it was the best of all the shows that year, 1985. That year he also

Olmos also played characters who went after outlaws. Here he is as Lieutenant Martin Castillo in the television series Miami Vice.

won an Emmy, the prestigious award for television acting. The next year he won a Golden Globe Award for Best Actor.

During this time Edward James Olmos was also recognized for his work with people. He won several Golden Eagle awards, given in Los Angeles every year to outstanding members of the Latino community.

Olmos holds one of his many Golden Eagle Awards for outstanding work in the Latino community.

Extending a message of hope and self-respect to teenagers during Christmas season, 1986.

Since he had starred in *Zoot Suit*, Olmos had been visiting public schools, community groups, prisons, and drug rehabilitation houses, in Los Angeles and elsewhere. He liked to talk to children and teenagers. They asked him how he got to be a famous actor. There are three things that help you be anything you want to be, he said. First, you have to have *patience:* Don't ever give up. Second, you have to have *faith:* Believe in yourself. And finally, it's important to have *dignity:* Be proud of yourself. Olmos felt proud if he could give integrity to ethnic experience. He wanted people to see that the Asian or Latino characters he played were real—people who were creative, intelligent, and had feelings.

Olmos instilled this same sense of integrity and discipline in his two sons, Mico and Bodie. (The boys were born during the early 1970s. They were young teenagers when Olmos appeared in *Miami Vice*.) Olmos and his sons also went on long bike rides together, sometimes as long as 20 miles (32 kilometers) a day, and as often as five days a week. His sons trained intensively because they were athletes. And they loved being outdoors and participating in sports. The family also enjoyed going out on the water in Olmos's speedboat, which he named *Bushido*. Olmos made so much money from his role on *Miami Vice* that he bought himself an expensive sports car. His sons thought that was very cool.

PORTRAYING CHICANO EXPERIENCE · In 1988, when the *Miami Vice* show ended, the Olmos family left Miami and moved back to Los Angeles. Edward James Olmos began making a movie called *Stand and Deliver*. Like *The Ballad of Gregorio Cortez*, it was based on a true story. It was about a Latino high school teacher in Los Angeles, Jaime Escalante, who believed that his Latino students were smart, even though other people said

Jaime Escalante (right) works with actor Lou Diamond Phillips while making the movie Stand and Deliver. *Olmos admired Escalante's dedication to his Chicano students.*

they weren't. This teacher worked with his students in class and even visited their homes, to help them prepare for tests that would get them into college. Escalante showed the students that he had faith in them. Olmos liked this story because the teacher had integrity and inspired young people.

Olmos's research for his part in *Stand and Deliver* was different from what he had done to prepare for parts in the past. Instead of reading about his character, he watched him. Olmos went to school each day with Jaime Escalante and observed how he taught his classes and how he visited with students. Olmos learned to imitate his gestures, and even had his hair shaved so that he looked like the balding Escalante. And Olmos also gained 40 pounds (18 kilograms) to resemble his character.

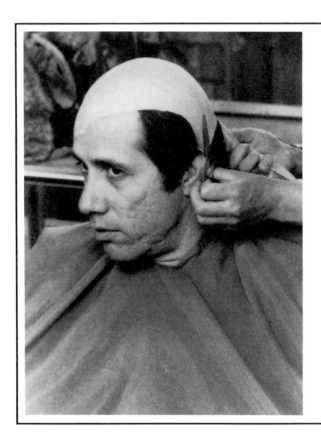

Olmos worked hard to portray Escalante. Here he is being made up to look like the balding high school teacher.

Soon Olmos felt like he *was* this East L.A. math teacher who motivated his unruly students to improve their grades. With this movie he showed viewers a possible reason why young people join gangs and hang out looking tough: Maybe it's because people treat them as if they are unable to do any better, just because they are Latinos.

The movie was shown both in theaters and on television. When people saw it, they praised it. Many called it one of the most inspiring movies they had ever seen. *Stand and Deliver* made millions of dollars, and Olmos got a nomination for an Oscar for Best Actor of the year.

In July of 1988, *Time* magazine chose Olmos to be on the cover of its special issue devoted to Latinos. Inside, article after article was about Latinos excelling in film, literature, dance, business, and a number of other professions. There was a long article about Olmos and how committed he was to performing good, positive roles in his acting. The article also explained that Olmos never drank alcohol or used drugs and was an important role model.

In 1990, Olmos started working on a script for another movie about Latinos, called *American Me.* It was about the younger generation of Chicano kids in the barrio, or neighborhood, of East L.A.—kids who didn't have many breaks in life, kids whose parents were

Members of a Chicano gang flash a special hand sign. Neglected in school, mistreated by police, many young Chicanos find safety and a sense of belonging in gangs. They find violent lifestyles and early deaths as well. Olmos presented these aspects of gang life in the movie American Me.

drug addicts or very poor. These kids got into gangs and spent most of their lives in prison. They didn't know how to be anything else.

Olmos decided to coproduce and direct this movie, besides playing the leading role. Olmos portrayed a young man in a gang who goes to jail as a teenager. When he is released, he has a difficult time adjusting to life and soon goes back to prison. He tries to stop members of his gang from killing other people in the prison. But they, in turn, kill him.

The character Olmos played in *American Me* wants to have a different life but cannot. His fate is sealed by poverty, ignorance, and prejudice. Olmos made this movie because he hoped people would help young Chicanos get out of this trap.

When the movie was released in 1992, many people criticized it for its violence. Many complained that Olmos's character had too much "macho," or tough Chicano male, attitude. Olmos said it was important to show how people lived. Chicanos were trying to win some respect for themselves and their community by acting tough, he said. The problem was that they were destroying themselves in the process.

Another aspect of gang life Olmos (center) showed in American Me *was prison, where conflicts begun on the streets continue behind bars.*

Helping to clean up Los Angeles after the 1992 riots.

THE LOS ANGELES RIOTS
AND EDWARD JAMES OLMOS

On April 29, 1992, a jury cleared three white Los Angeles police officers charged with beating Rodney King, a black man, during an arrest. (A fourth white officer was also charged with beating King. The jury could not decide his case.) People around the country had seen a videotape of the arrest. To many, it offered proof that the officers had brutally kicked and beaten King.

The verdict sparked a riot. People in Los Angeles's black and Hispanic neighborhoods set fires, broke into businesses, and stole and destroyed property. Community leaders took to the streets to try to stop the violence. One of the first on the scene was Edward James Olmos. Olmos made daily trips to the riot areas and talked to people. He tried to make them understand that the only way to solve problems was to work together—not to destroy each other.

When the riots ended, Olmos joined an organization called Rebuilding Los Angeles. He helped business owners clean up and rebuild their stores. Even while working on a movie more than a year later, he made frequent trips to Los Angeles to encourage people to get along.

Edward James Olmos appears with a red ribbon in this photo. The purpose of the red ribbon is to make people more aware of AIDS, and of the need to find a cure for the disease.

Olmos produced a documentary on the making of *American Me*, called *Lives in Hazard*, in 1994. He then began work on a new movie about Chicano farm workers. Olmos also remarried in 1994. (He had divorced Kaija some time earlier.) His second wife was Lorraine Bracco.

PURSUING DREAMS · Olmos said he would continue working on movies about characters with integrity. One character Olmos wanted to play was Don Quixote, the most famous character in Spanish literature. Don Quixote was a knight who pursued his dreams.

When he was a child, Olmos was impatient to find the secret to making dreams come true. He would always pester his dad to tell him how. One day, tired of his questioning, his father ordered: *"¡Siéntate!"* ("Sit down!") Then he said, *"Mi hijo* [my son], you are born to die, and in between, life asks but one question: Are you happy?"

When Eddie was twelve he thought that didn't mean anything. But he learned that it did. He grew to understand that happiness was doing what you believed in. "If you can be happy every day of your life, then you have *done* something," he said. "I come from a divorced family. I'm a minority. I have no natural talent, but I did what was important to me. I've *done* something, and I'm happy."

IMPORTANT DATES IN
EDWARD JAMES OLMOS'S LIFE

1947 Olmos is born in East Los Angeles, California, on February 24.

1969 Marries Kaija Keel.

1978 Wins the Los Angeles Drama Critics Circle Award for his portrayal of El Pachuco in *Zoot Suit*. He is also nominated for a Tony Award.

1985 Wins the Emmy Award for Best Supporting Actor in *Miami Vice*.

1986 Wins a Golden Globe Award for Best Actor in *Miami Vice*.

1988 Is nominated for an Oscar for Best Actor in the movie *Stand and Deliver*. He appears on the cover of the July 11 issue of *Time* magazine.

1992 Coproduces and directs his own movie, *American Me*.

1994 Produces a documentary, *Lives in Hazard*, about the making of *American Me*. Marries Lorraine Bracco.

FIND OUT MORE
ABOUT ACTING

The Good Apple Guide to Creative Drama by Kathryn Foley. Carthage, Ill.: Good Apple, 1981.

Monologues for Kids by Ruth M. Roddy. Toluca Lake, Calif.: Dramaline, 1987.

FIND OUT MORE
ABOUT MEXICAN-AMERICANS

Hector Lives in the United States Now: The Story of a Mexican-American Child by Joan Hewett. New York: HarperCollins, 1990.

Hello Amigos! by Tricia Brown. New York: Holt, 1986.

Portraits of Mexican Americans by Nancy Marquez and Theresa Perez. Carthage, Ill.: Good Apple, 1991.

INDEX

Page numbers in *italics* refer to illustrations.